The Promised Land

Scripture text from
The Contemporary English Version

Master Books

CHAPTER • 1

Joshua, the Successor of Moses

This Flemish miniature presents Joshua, the successor of Moses. He is majestic in his vivid clothing. In one hand he holds a viola-like musical instrument, while in the other, he has the bow. This is not the conquering Joshua, but the great leader of the Israelites, peaceful and levelheaded, perhaps *after* reaching the Promised Land.

Flemish medieval art, miniature **Lambertus:** "Liber Floridus," Apocalypse God in Glory, The Prophets (ms 724/1596 fol. 10 #1 circa 1448 [detail] Joshua.)

© Giraudon - Condé Museum, Chantilly (France)

The Promised Land at Last

The Jordan

The Israelites who had left Egypt with Moses crossed a dry and endless desert. After a long walk and many stops, they arrived at the River Jordan. Their leader, Moses, had earlier died and the young Joshua had replaced him. For a long time the Israelites had dreamed of a better land. They remembered what God had promised their ancestor Abraham – countless descendants and a plentiful land "flowing with milk and honey." Now it seems that the promise is about to come true. They are now at a point where they can actually see the land just beyond the Jordan.* Compared with the dry desert, the Promised Land looks like a rich and fertile garden. It is a true paradise.

The people find mountains, valleys, fertile plains, water and forests in the new land. But they also find the land is already occupied by other people called "Canaanites," because the land was known as "Canaan."

We know today that people had lived in that land from very ancient times. Around 1150 B.C. when the Israelites entered the land, the Canaanites had cultivated fertile fields. They lived in small, fortified cities. They worshiped the god Baal and his companion, the goddess Astarte.** The lives of the Canaanites would soon be changed by the settling of the Israelites.

Photo of the Sinai Desert

A Land Given by God

The book of Joshua*** tells about the settlements of the Israelites in Canaan. Joshua himself recorded these events so that we would have a true and accurate account of Israelite history, as they conquered an idolatrous people. This book shows the reader that Canaan is the land that God had promised to Abraham and that they are among the countless descendants of Abraham, Isaac, and Jacob. That's why Joshua began the book with the Lord's words: "Long ago I promised the ancestors of Israel that I would give this land to their descendants...I am the Lord your God, and I will be there to help you wherever you go." (Joshua 6:9).

* Jordan
The Jordan is the major river in Israel. It flows from the north to the south and ends in the Dead Sea. It forms the border between Israel and Jordan.

** Baal and Astarte
These were the gods worshiped by the Canaanites. They were believed to make plants grow and give good harvests.

*** The Book of Joshua
The sixth book of the Bible. It tells the story of the Israelites' settlement into Canaan and the division of the land among the twelve tribes of Israel.

So Be Strong and Brave!

Joshua 1.1-9 (excerpts)

Moses, the LORD's servant, was dead. So the LORD spoke to Joshua... who had been the assistant of Moses. The LORD said:...

My servant Moses is dead. Now you must lead Israel across the Jordan River into the land I'm giving to all of you. Wherever you go, I'll give you that land, as I promised Moses. It will reach from the Southern Desert to the Lebanon Mountains in the north, and to the northeast as far as the great Euphrates River.... I will always be with you and help you as I helped Moses, and no one will ever be able to defeat you.

Long ago I promised the ancestors of Israel that I would give this land to their descendants. So be strong and brave! Be careful to do everything my servant Moses taught you. Never stop reading *The Book of the Law* he gave you. Day and night you must think about what it says. If you obey it completely, you and Israel will be able to take this land.

I've commanded you to be strong and brave. Don't ever be afraid or discouraged! I am the LORD your God, and I will be there to help you wherever you go.

Joshua

In Hebrew, "Joshua" is pronounced *Yehoshoua*. This name means "God saves" or "God frees." It was also the Hebrew name given to Jesus.

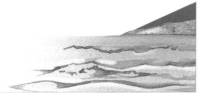

The Euphrates River

The Euphrates lay east of Canaan, far beyond the river Jordan, and originally formed the border of the land. The prophecy foretells the time when David will extend the borders of Israel.

I Promised

The Book of Genesis tells of the promise God made to Abraham: *"I will give this land to your family forever."* (Genesis 12.7)

5

The Desired Land

The Dream of a Country

People who have been forced to live outside their homeland must dream of living in their own country again someday. Other people are forced to leave everything behind and flee to a safer place only to have to submit to foreign rulers. They all dream of resettling in their own country where they can finally build a house, enjoy the company of good neighbors, rear their children, and live in peace and be free!

Promise

God promises to help and be with his children, especially those who are suffering. God supports them in their desire to live under his laws — which is the true homeland of those who love God. God gives them insight to recognize right from wrong and encourages them to live in harmony with each other.

Wars

God wants nothing to do with violence. Sometimes people have used the name of God to justify their wars or their oppression of others. God is not a warrior. Rather, God is a God of Peace and Love. How could a peaceful and loving God be on the side of those who bring about death? No war is holy. War is always a work of death.

Perfect Homeland?

No land or country is a perfect. Everyone knows that. Yet, in spite of it, people love their country and are proud to claim, "It's my country. It's my home. This is my family!" Those who live away from their homeland often dream of returning to it to live there among those they love.

One Earth for All

God entrusts the earth to all humans for their happiness. Therefore it is everyone's responsibility to share the land so that each nation can be independent and free. No nation has the right to take the land of another. It is the duty of nations to see that no one is deprived of the fundamental right to a homeland.

Be Strong

Sometimes difficulties
Arise one after
The other: a broken friendship,
A split family,
The death of a loved one,
Mourning and sorrow, illness
With its parade of suffering...

How can one not give up
When facing the avalanche of sadness?

Sometimes the events of the world
Occur in the sound of fury:
Hatred between people,
Weapons of death
Built without any scruples, only
For economic profit,
Wars starting over...

How can anyone not avoid being drawn
To discouragement
When facing the human impossibility
Of building together a happy earth?

God promises his presence
God faithfully promises
Land to all his children:
"Be strong!"
He remains by their side
In the heart of difficulties
And terrible events.
He communicates to them
The strength of his Spirit
So that they can keep on
Believing in happiness
And make it come true!

CHAPTER 2

Jericho, the Door into Canaan

The miniaturist Jean Fouquet presents the triumphal entrance of Joshua and the children of Israel into the city of Jericho. His artistic style alternates between naturalism (realism) and mannerism (artificiality). The landscapes, the architecture of the city, and the clothing of the characters are all very detailed. The parade in the foreground is lively and brilliant with color. The Sacred Chest of the Agreement and the golden trumpets glow.

Jean Fouquet
(circa 1420-1481)
Flavius Josephus: "Judaic Antiquities." The Fall of Jericho
(ms. fr. 247, Volume 1 fol. 80)

© Tearci - Giraudon/National Library of France, Paris (France)

The Crossing

The ruins of Jericho

How did the children of Israel enter Canaan? Moses had led the people to an area east of the river Jordan. God would not allow Moses to enter into the Promised Land with the people, but did let him view it from Mt. Nebo. After Moses died, Joshua prepared the people to enter the land, which was inhabited by many pagans who worshipped nature and stone and wood idols.

The Canaanites and Jebusites who occupied the land had built fortified cities and the task of conquering them looked hopeless. The enemies were powerful. But Joshua trusted the Lord.

In a truly great miraculous way, God helped the Israelites in their first confrontation with the people of the land. At Jericho*, God instructed his people to march around the city and then blow trumpets. When they obeyed, the walls fell down flat and the Israelites saw again that their God was the true deity, all-powerful and capable of smashing the false idols from Canaan. The "door" to the Promised Land had been opened in a dramatic way!

Statue of a flute player from Rome in Italy

At the Sound of Trumpets

The Book of Joshua recalls the vivid account of the fall of Jericho. It is a true story of faithfulness. In addition to possessing the land and cities, God commanded the Israelites to destroy the inhabitants, who had engaged in much evil. The Canaanites, as recorded in the Bible, even sacrificed their own children by burning them as an offering to the gods. Modern archaeology has shown this to be true. Truly, God was calling his people to have nothing to do with such evil. Jericho reminds us today that God judges and punishes sin. Evil may flourish for awhile, but God's justice triumphs in the end.

*Jericho
The city of Jericho has ten levels of occupation that have recently been excavated. This makes it one of the oldest cities in the world. It is located near an oasis east of Canaan, close to the Jordan River.

The Walls of Jericho

Joshua 6.1-16 (excerpts)

The people of Jericho had been locking the gates in their town wall because they were afraid of the Israelites. No one could go out or come in.

The LORD said to Joshua:

With my help, you and your army will defeat the king of Jericho and his army, and you will capture the town. Here is how to do it: March slowly around Jericho once a day for six days. Take along the sacred chest and have seven priests walk in front of it, carrying trumpets.

But on the seventh day, march slowly around the town seven times while the priests blow their trumpets. Then the priests will blast on their trumpets, and everyone else will shout. The wall will fall down, and your soldiers can go straight in from every side....

They obeyed Joshua's orders and carried the chest once around the town before returning to camp for the night.

They did this once a day for six days.

On the seventh day, the army got up at daybreak. They marched slowly around Jericho the same as they had done for the past six days, except on this day they went around seven times. Then the priests blew the trumpets, and Joshua yelled:

Get ready to shout! The LORD will let you capture this town.

The King of Jericho

In Canaan each city had its own king who was the leader of the city. There were more than thirty cities in the country.

Seven

The number seven is considered sacred. It comes up often in the Bible; for instance, the seven days of creation and the seven priests encircling Jericho.

Trumpets

The trumpet was a musical instrument that was used on two occasions – to call men to battle and to praise God during a religious ceremony.

The Walls Come Tumbling Down!

Always Further

Life sometimes seem to be a long journey marked by both challenges and joys. Challenges and obstacles can sometimes seem so overwhelming that people are tempted to close themselves off from the outside world and from others. What is the point of making efforts if they don't lead to success? Yet God calls people to keep on going no matter what, to keep hoping for progress, and to learn to grow in the midst of their difficulties.

Wins and Losses

Isn't life sometimes a struggle? Aren't we called to overcome our shortcomings, offer only our good qualities, fight against our selfishness, and control the unkindness that harms others with our speech and actions? We must be able to recognize that our struggles will result in some wins and some losses. The stories we read in the books of Joshua and Judges can teach us the importance of never giving in to hopelessness and defeat.

Fortresses

When Jesus promised us that the gates of hell would not prevail against his people, he was telling us that no obstacle is too strong for God. Nothing can hamper God in his plan to redeem mankind; no problem is too tall. We can have assurance that God is with us in all circumstances, even as he was with the Israelites who stood at the high walls of Jericho.

The Promised Land

The Promised Land is not some fantasyland of long ago. The Promised Land was given to the children of Israel forever. Although we are grieved at the fighting going on there today, we know that God's promises are sure. Many Christians also view their heavenly reward as the "Promised Land," where pain and suffering will be no more!

Unity

Jesus calls his Church to rock-solid unity, gathering around the great truth and hope that Christ is the light of the world — the savior who came because all have sinned and fallen short of God's standard.

Sacred Stewardship

God entrusts Christians
to "occupy until he comes."

They are responsible for
conserving earth's resources.
They are in charge
of caring for animals
and wilderness areas.

They are to care
for the weak, the naked,
the poor, the hungry
of the world.
They are to resist
using resources and
people for their own
selfish gain,
so that all have
enough.

They are responsible
for telling others
that lasting peace
is not built by man,
but must await the
coming of Jesus
and his kingdom.

If all human beings
followed the laws
of God, think what
a wonderful home
we would have!

The Agreement at Shechem

In this bas-relief sculpture, the Canaanite god Baal is shown with thunder. The Hebrew word *Baal* actually means "lord." It was used to refer to several gods that were the patron deities of cities. Pictured here is the storm god Hadad holding a thunderbolt in his right hand. He is wearing a pointed hat and has a beard. In the Bible, the term *Baal* refers to all false gods.

Stela of Baal, nineteenth century B.C., Ram Shamra in Syria.

To Live in Canaan

H i s t o r y

Peruvian man tying up strands of reed

Now that the Israelites are settled in Canaan, many things are different… and not always easy. They had lived in tents; now must learn to build houses. They used to move around freely, carrying their tents with them; now they must learn to live in and around villages. They had made their living by herding sheep and goats; now they must learn to farm the ground. They had marched together in family groups; now the tribes* are scattered throughout the country, each with its own territory.** They had been used to thinking of themselves as one people under the direction of the LORD; now they are separated and intermingled among native inhabitants with their own customs and laws. They had been faithful to the Lord their God; now they observe the Canaanites worshiping Baal and Astarte, the gods of fertile ground and plentiful harvests. The Israelites wonder to themselves: "To have good harvests, do we also need to worship the god and goddess of this land?"

The Union of the Tribes

Joshua is concerned about the temptation of the Israelites to worship the Canaanite gods. To encourage his people to remain faithful to the God of Abraham and Moses, he calls them to Shechem***, a city located in central Canaan. He reminds them of their past history and about the Lord their God who led them out of slavery in Egypt and gave them the gift of the land of Canaan. He then asks them to choose freely between their God and the gods of the other people.

The people make an agreement to be faithful to their God over the Canaanite gods. Their choice is another step in preserving the agreement God had made with their ancestors.

As the Bible tells the history of Israel, we read of various agreements that God made and renewed with the Israelites. The agreement at Shechem is one of these. Others will follow.

Man from Guatemala building the walls to his house

* The tribes
The Israelites are divided into different groups: clans, families, and tribes. The tribes are called by the names of the twelve sons of Jacob. For example, there is the Judah tribe and the Ephraim tribe.

** Throughout the country
The Book of Joshua tells us that the land was divided among the following tribes: Reuben, Gad, Manasseh, Judah, Ephraim, Benjamin, Simeon, Zebulun, Issachar, Asher, Naphtali, and Dan. These tribal territories can be seen on the map on page 35.

*** Shechem
Shechem is an ancient city located between mountains. It was here that the children of Israel buried the bones of Joseph, which they had carried up from Egypt. This fulfilled the request Joseph made just before he died.

15

Bible

To Choose the Lord

Joshua 24.1-28 (excerpts)

Joshua called the tribes of Israel together for a meeting at Shechem. He had the leaders, including the old men, the judges, and the officials, come up and stand near the sacred tent. Then Joshua told everyone to listen to this message from the LORD, the God of Israel:

… You didn't have to work for this land – I gave it to you. Now you live in towns you didn't build, and you eat grapes and olives from vineyards and trees you didn't plant.

Then Joshua told the people:

Worship the LORD, obey him, and always be faithful. Get rid of the idols your ancestors worshiped…. But if you don't want to worship the LORD, then choose right now! Will you worship the same idols your ancestors did? Or since you're living on land that once belonged to the Amorites, maybe you'll worship their gods. I won't. My family and I are going to worship and obey the LORD!

The people answered:

We could never worship other gods or stop worshiping the LORD. The LORD is our God. We were slaves in Egypt as our ancestors had been, but we saw the LORD work miracles to set our people free and to bring us out of Egypt…. Yes, we will worship and obey the LORD, because the LORD is our God.

Joshua helped Israel make an agreement with the LORD that day at Shechem. Joshua made laws for Israel and wrote them down in *The Book of the Law of God*. Joshua sent everyone back to their homes.

The God of Israel

Quite apart from the thousands of clay, wood, and stone idols worshipped by the previous inhabitants of Canaan, the Israelites knew and understood that Jehovah was the only true God, the maker of heaven and earth. Sadly, they mixed with some pagan peoples and began worshipping false gods.

Choose Right Now!

In the Bible it is usually God who chooses his people. This text is an exception. It is Israel that needs to choose its LORD.

The Amorites

This name was used for the people who lived in Canaan before the arrival of the Israelites. The Amorites probably lived in the mountains and the Canaanites, in the plains.

To Live Together

To Live Together

There are so many nations, cultures, religions, and political boundaries that can divide people into unshakeable categories! How can we learn to live together without being jealous or resentful of others and without trying to impose laws on others? If we are to live at peace with others, everyone must have an opportunity to speak. We must learn to listen, to show respect to others, and to try to find points of agreement – despite our differences.

To Remain United

It is possible for human beings to exist together as a family. It is not just an impossible dream! People are capable of thinking of others as equals and of finding peaceful solutions to their conflicts. We have God's Spirit working in us to strive for understanding and peace among peoples and nations. When we work toward peace, God is truly among us!

Idols

People are inclined to worship the various false gods or idols they create for themselves. These may include money, fashion, financial success, things, astrology, fame, or sports. Many people around us are prisoners of these idols because they depend on them for meaning and even dedicate their whole lives to getting and keeping them.

To Remain Faithful

People are sometimes tempted to drift away from God. They forget God and believe they can achieve happiness through their own efforts! True happiness is found in faithfulness to God. To be faithful to God means living the way God wants us to: loving God and loving others. Our obedience to God derives out of our gratitude for what God has done for us.

Sacred Agreement

It is important to remember the agreement that God has made with us, the people of God. And it is important to acknowledge God by saying: "You are my God!" It is also important to gather regularly to say together: "We choose to believe in God! Without God, we are lost."

They Choose

They choose
to acknowledge God
as the creator of life.

They choose
to put all their trust in him.

They choose
to call him Father
and to live as his children.

They choose
to consider that
he sent a Savior.

They choose
to be faithful to God and to let
his word enlighten
the winding paths of their existence.

They choose
to thank God
all their days
for the love
he has given
in his son, Jesus.

They choose
to fight against the evil
that tries to divert them from him
and tries to destroy the
work of spreading
the Gospel.

The Liberating Judges

The Italian artist, Francesco Solimena, from Naples was a key figure of the Baroque period, which was somewhat excessive in its art forms. He presents the story of Deborah and Barak in a large fresco, a painting done on fresh, moist plaster. The power of this scene is the result of the attitudes of the characters and the vivid colors in their clothing. In spite of a tendency towards classicism or traditional art forms, the painting on the whole bears witness to the fiery style and passion of the artist.

Francesco Solimena
(1657-1747),
Barak and Deborah,
Italy

© Giraudon / Collection of the Duke of Harrach, Vienna (Austria)

A Very Hard Period

Mount Tabor

For almost 150 years, life for the Israelites who settled in Canaan was very hard. Besides having to adapt to new situations, they also had to defend themselves against enemies. On the east, the Philistines* troubled their borders. To the south, the king of Moab charged the children of Israel heavy taxes. In the central area, Israel was at the mercy of raids by the Midianites** who came from the desert. In the north, Canaanite princes threatened the unity of the tribes.

But God does not let Israel be defeated. Whenever there is danger, God raises up special leaders to help them. These gifted leaders are called "Judges" or "Liberators." They gather troops from the tribes to defend the territory or tribes under attack or threatened. The people recognize that the Lord sent the Judges.

Statue from Vienna, Austria

The Book of Judges

This book, the seventh of the Bible, recalls the memory of these troubled times. It tells the story of the difficulties and oppression*** suffered by the Israelites even in the Promised Land. It describes the actions of the liberators, the "Judges," who were directed by the Spirit of the Lord. Among them is Deborah, the only female Judge, but who was one of the most important.

Deborah appoints Barak as the general to gather and lead the Israelite troops against the Canaanites who threaten to cut off the northern tribes from the rest of Israel's tribes. The poorly armed Israelites are victorious over an enemy that is much more powerful than they. How is this possible? The Bible tells us that God stopped the Canaanite chariots and that the Israelites used their swords to kill the fleeing enemy. For Israel it is clear that the Lord has fought for them.

* Philistines
The people known as the Philistines arrived in Canaan from the Mediterranean Sea (in the west) about the same time as the Israelites came from the desert (in the east). The Philistines settled along the shore and made regular attacks on the Israelite tribes for more land.

** Midianites
The Midianites were powerful nomads who lived in the desert. They rode camels so they could move quickly and travel long distances.

*** Oppression
The book of Joshua equates oppression of the Israelites with their unfaithfulness to the Lord their God. But after they admit their sin and call upon the Lord, God sends them a Judge to lead them into victory and freedom.

B i b l e

Deborah and Barak

Judges 4.4-16; 5.1-31 (excerpts)

Deborah the wife of Lappidoth was a prophet and a leader of Israel during those days…
She said:

I have a message for you from the LORD God of Israel! You are to get together an army of ten thousand men…and lead them to Mount Tabor. The LORD will trick Sisera into coming out to fight you at the Kishon River. Sisera will be leading King Jabin's army as usual, and they will have their chariots, but the LORD has promised to help you defeat them….

When Sisera learned that Barak had led an army to Mount Tabor, he called his troops together and got all nine hundred iron chariots ready. Then he led his army away from Harosheth-Ha-Goiim to the Kishon River.

Deborah shouted, "Barak, it's time to attack Sisera! Because today the LORD is gong to help you defeat him. In fact, the LORD has already gone on ahead to fight for you."

Barak led his ten thousand troops down from Mount Tabor. And during the battle, the LORD confused Sisera, his chariot drivers, and his whole army. Everyone was so afraid of Barak and his army, that even Sisera jumped down from his chariot and tried to escape….

Sisera's entire army was wiped out.

After the battle… Deborah and Barak sang this song:

Listen, kings and rulers,
while I sing for the LORD,
        the God of Israel….
Rain poured from the sky,
the earth trembled,
        and mountains shook.
The LORD's people who were left
joined with their leaders
        and fought at my side….
Canaanite kings fought us…
but they couldn't rob us
        of our silver.
From their pathways in the sky
        the stars fought Sisera,
and his soldiers were swept away
        by the ancient Kishon River….
Our LORD, we pray
that all your enemies
        will die like Sisera.
But let everyone who loves you
shine brightly like the sun
        at dawn.

Deborah

Deborah is one of the great women of the Bible. She is a prophet, and a victorious Judge. Her name means "the bee." She stings the enemies of Israel until they are forced to retreat.

The Kishon River

This victory in Israel reflects a similar event at the earlier departure from Egypt. There, Pharoah's army perished in the Red Sea. A century after the flight from Egypt the chariots of Sisera, the general of the enemy army, also become useless.

Enemies

At the time of the Judges, anyone who was an enemy of Israel was considered an enemy of the LORD God.

To Live Freely

True Liberty

Does God hold us in his hand, or do we put our faith in idols? We are not so different from ancient peoples, those who thought that maybe God is not really so powerful, or maybe he has an equal. This sin, condemned in the time of Moses, has never really left us. It is still up to us to choose: God, or gods?

Troubled Times

In times of change, people often find themselves troubled. Should a person continue to cling to the old ways, or is it better to adapt to the new? While good in their time, older ways sometimes don't seem to meet modern needs. Yet newer ways often present problems that we don't yet know how to solve. Believers must ask themselves, "In this time of change, what ways will help us grow? Which changes does God want us to welcome and which should we reject?"

Strength

To be strong does not consist only of the use of muscles or the use of force to order others around and overpower them. Strength of character has nothing to do with power in this sense. Being strong also means not feeling overwhelmed or worried when change comes. In this sense, being strong derives from an unchanging faith in God.

To Turn toward God

In troubled times, just as in times of peace, believers turn to God and remain attentive to God's call. Each day they remain aware of God's faithful presence and steadfast love, on which they know they can lean.

Rights and Duties

When conquerors attack or dictators deprive others of their freedom, people often rise up to defend their life and liberty. It is their right… and even their duty! During times of oppression, people often pray to God to support those who are persecuted for trying to gain freedom for themselves or others. They strive to change the evil in people's hearts.

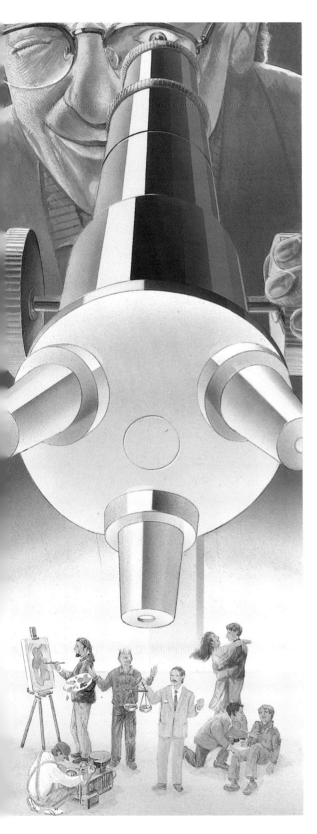

Searchers of Signs

Where is he, God?
Does he really accompany
the long walk of humanity?

Only those who search
are capable of distinguishing
the signs of his presence
and his intervention
in human history!

The searchers find the signs of God
in undertakings of solidarity,
in the humanity that moves toward
equal justice for all,
in the beauty
created by the genius of artists,
in the inventions
that cure sickness,
in prayer that shows faith in God,
in the smile of tenderness,
in the forgiveness that renews bonds,
and in the love that is greater
than the stingiest selfishness.

The searchers of signs know –
these works are so great
that only the Spirit of God
could inspire them
in the human heart!

Judges or a King?

In this painting, Samson sleeps at the feet of Delilah, a Philistine woman. She puts a finger to her lips to remind the surrounding people to be silent. In her hand she holds scissors. She is ready to cut Samson's hair, which she now knows is the source of his strength. Her face appears soft and calm, although she is about to betray Samson.

Giuseppe Nuvolone (1619-1703), "Samson and Delilah," Italy
© Giraudon - Museum of Fine Arts, Caen (France)

Twelve Judges

Statue of a Judge from Athens, Greece

The book of Judges tells about twelve* of Israel's liberators. The accounts of their deeds, heroic and amazing in their faithfulness, were preserved to encourage generations of God's people in the face of persecution. One of these judges, Ehud, used trickery to kill an enemy from the south, the king of Moab. Gideon the judge penetrates a camp of raiding Midianites with only 300 men! Another judge, Jephthah, defeats the powerful Ammonites.

The strong man Samson** plays tricks on the Philistines and goes on to be betrayed by Delilah. These histories have been preserved for us today, and to help the children of Israel remember their past and strengthen their faith in the Lord.

A King, Why Not?

Even with the success of its judges, Israel remained weak in comparison with surrounding nations. Unlike its neighbors, Israel was not organized under a single leader. A king, who reigns for many years, provides a stable government and has the authority to organize a national army. A king unites the people, whereas some of Israel's judges acted on behalf of only a few select tribes. Once the armies achieved victory over their enemies, they returned to their own territory.

So certain voices called out, "We want a king like the other nations!" But others answered, "No! The Lord God is our King!" Those who opposed the establishment of a monarchy (kingdom) told a fable (see next page) to show the danger in having a king.

But in the end Israel did have a king. The first king of Israel was Saul.*** Another new step had been taken in the history of Israel.

* Twelve
Just as there are twelve tribes of Israel (and later, twelve apostles of Jesus) there are twelve judges who are remembered in the book of Judges.

** Samson
People believed that Samson's strength was his long hair. Not cutting one's hair was considered a sign of one's dedication to God.

*** Saul
Saul was the first king of Israel. At the request of the people, the prophet/judge Samuel anointed him. Later, Saul is killed in a battle against the Philistines and replaced by David.

B i b l e

The Fable of Trees

Judges 9.8-15

Once the trees searched
        for someone to be king;
they asked the olive tree,
        "Will you be our king?"
But the olive tree replied,
"My oil brings honor
        to people and gods.
I won't stop making oil,
just to have my branches wave
        above the other trees."
Then they asked the fig tree,
        "Will you be our king?"
But the fig tree replied,
"I won't stop growing
            my delicious fruit,
        just to have my branches wave
            above the other trees."

Next they asked the grape vine,
        "Will you be our king?"
But the grape vine replied,
"My wine brings cheer
        to people and gods.
I won't stop making wine,
just to have my branches wave
        above the other trees."
Finally, they went
to the thornbush and asked,
"Will you be our king?"
The thornbush replied,
"If you really want me,
        to be your king,
then come into my shade
        and I will protect you.

But if you're deceiving me,
    I'll start a fire
that will spread out and destroy
    the cedars of Lebanon."

They Asked

This fable is not about pantheism, the wrong belief that God is in trees or natural objects.

The Thornbush

In contrast with the other trees (olive tree, fig tree, grapevine), the thornbush does not produce fruit. It also possesses piercing thorns. Useless and dangerous, it gives a true picture of an evil king.

The Cedars of Lebanon

The cedar tree is the most majestic of trees in the Middle East. In the fable, the cedar is outside the surroundings of the other trees, yet the thornbush draws the stately cedar into its drive for power. The lesson is that the action of a bad king can reach even beyond the borders of his country.

Those Who Remain Aware of God's Presence among Them Will Have Always a Source of Hope

Examples

Everyone needs examples by which to live, believe, love, and hope. It is important to remember men and women who resisted evil during their lives, who kept their faith in God, who gave their lives for others, and who refused to lose hope. They are models who call us to be open to progress. They demonstrate unshakable faith in God.

Bold

Other people help us hold on to our hope. Some lived in the past, while others are alive today. Their example stirs our courage to rise above selfishness and evil. They show us that in spite of difficulties, we can make extraordinary things happen.

True Saints

We all know people who behaved as saints, and the Church recognizes several others. These saints focused their strength on the practice of loving God and loving others. They remind us of the possibilities that come about when we remain faithful to our agreement with God. They spur us on to believe in God who remains with us always, bringing freedom and abundant life to all.

Change of Heart

The first and most important changes we need to make are always those within our own hearts. Above all, it's the heart that must be changed, for it is in the core of our being that jealousy, hatred, violence, refusal to love, and deceit take root. To free our heart is not easy. It requires effort, but God offers us help.

Royalty or Republic

Even though the Bible makes no recommendation about the best system of government, it does criticize oppressive leaders and rulers. The Bible exhorts all leaders to rule with justice and fairness, to respect all people as the image of God, and to share the earth equitably.

To Order or To Serve

Some are chosen
to govern.

If they behave
like authoritarian lords
who take everything for themselves
or like commanders
who demand blind obedience
or like dominating masters
who require slavish submission,
they don't properly fulfill their role,
they don't deserve their position
they are unfaithful to their mission.

Those who are chosen to govern
have one duty – to serve, to place themselves
at the call of their charges.

Good leaders devote their time
and their strength to helping their neighbor
win their daily bread
gain the respect of others
and live in dignity.
They listen and consult before
making decisions. They are careful that
no one is excluded or forgotten
in poverty.
They give of themselves
without counting the cost
so that happiness
may be shared by all
in a land of fellowship.

They hold that to serve
is their responsibility!

The Promised Land Today

You Can Go There

View of the city of Jerusalem

The country that the Bible calls the Promised Land still exists. It is known as Israel. You can go there for a visit. Perhaps someday you'll take a trip! It's a small country with only a little over five million inhabitants. It could fit into the United States about 450 times.

Numerous Pilgrims

Many believers go on pilgrimages to the Holy Land.

•Christians want to experience being in the very country where Jesus walked. Hundreds of thousands of pilgrims visit Bethlehem and Jerusalem every year to celebrate Christmas or Easter.

•Jews want to visit the land of their ancestors and the State of Israel that was founded in 1948. They pray at the Western Wall of the old Temple, destroyed by the Romans in A.D. 70. These pilgrims want to remember the history of this land and find hope for the future. The Jewish connection to the land is so strong that many people leave lucrative businesses all over the world to settle in the land of Israel. Truly, the words of the prophets are being fulfilled in our time.

A Painful Discovery

People who visit the Holy Land start out with faith, deep love of their religious traditions, and high expectations of being inspired. They quickly discover, however, that the present inhabitants of the Promised Land are embroiled in turmoil. The country suffers from ancient hatreds directed at the Jewish people. The Palestinian in-tifada, or uprising, began in 1987 and led to the Oslo Peace Accords. Sadly, efforts to build a permanent peace agreement have failed to curb these acts of violence and terror. Much effort has been put forth by world governments

Mosque of Hebron, sheltering Abraham' tomb

and the United Nations in trying to bring peace to the Middle East, but terrorist bombings and violent rhetoric still dominate the region. Regrettably, today the Promised Land is a land of division instead of love.

Signs of Hope

Various efforts at peace have failed, but the Bible is a sure source of truth and in it we are told (in the books of the prophets) that one day, Messiah will come to Jerusalem and bring lasting peace to the place that has seen violence for thousands of years. Although this sounds crazy to most people, it is the assurance we have from God.

The Oasis of Peace

The city of Jerusalem has been fought over for thousands of years. After he reigned at Hebron for seven years as king of Israel, David took the city from the Jebusites and established Jerusalem as Israel's eternal capital. Since his death, many wars have been fought in the region, and Jerusalem itself has been beseiged by the Assyrians, Babylonians, Romans, and modern armies. In June, 1967, the Israel Defense Forces liberated the city from the Jordanian army, thus calling to mind Jesus' words in Luke 21:24: "Jerusalem will be trampled on by the Gentiles until the times of the Gentiles are fulfilled."

This "city of peace" that has so captivated the world will one day be the seat of the Messiah, who Zechariah tells us will descend from heaven to the Mount of Olives (just to the east of today's Old City) and then take up his rightful place. Many people mock the words of the Bible and call it irrelevant, but all the peace efforts of men are being shown to be pitiful and inferior to the plans of the King of Peace.

Titles already published:

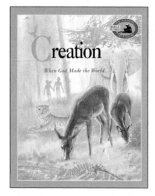

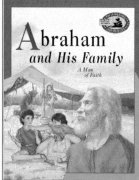

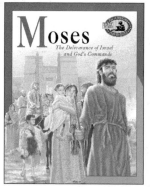

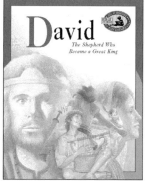

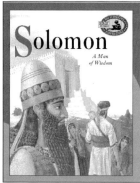

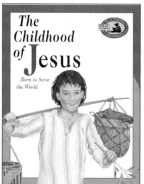

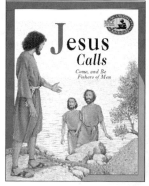

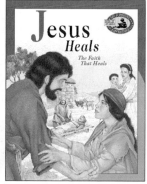

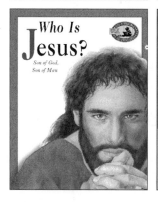

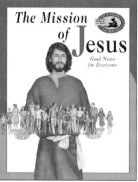

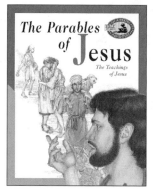

Forthcoming titles in the JUNIOR BIBLE Collection:

- The First Prophets
- Passion and Resurrection
- Exile and Return
- Isaiah, Micah, Jeremiah
- Jesus and the Outcasts
- Jesus in Jerusalem
- Acts
- Wisdom
- Psalms
- Women
- Revelation
- Letters

The Land of Canaan

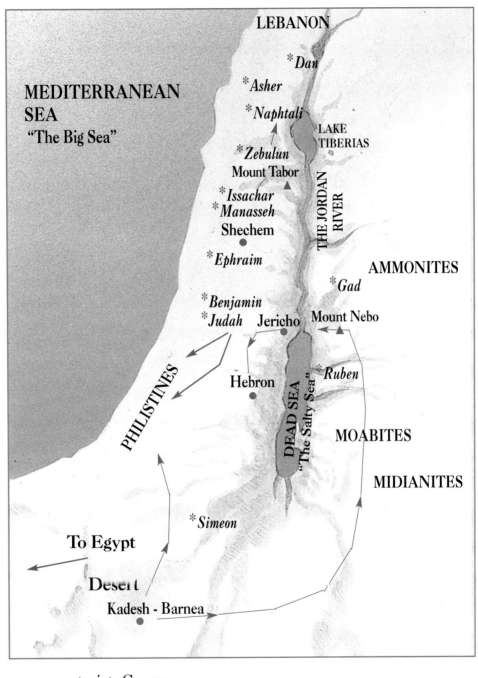

LEBANON

MEDITERRANEAN
SEA
"The Big Sea"

*Dan

*Asher

*Naphtali

LAKE
TIBERIAS

*Zebulun
Mount Tabor

THE JORDAN RIVER

*Issachar
*Manasseh
Shechem

*Ephraim

AMMONITES

*Gad

*Benjamin
*Judah   Jericho   Mount Nebo

PHILISTINES

Hebron

*Ruben

DEAD SEA
"The Salty Sea"

MOABITES

MIDIANITES

*Simeon

To Egypt

Desert

Kadesh - Barnea

⟶ : routes into Canaan

* : tribes of Israel

● : cities

0   20   40   60 miles

The
Promised
Land

ORIGINAL TEXT BY

Meredith HARTMAN, Karim BERRADA,

Loretta PASTVA, SND,

Albert HARI, Charles SINGER

ENGLISH TEXT ADAPTED BY

the American Bible Society

PHOTOGRAPHY

Frantisek ZVARDON

ILLUSTRATORS

Mariano VALSESIA, Betti FERRERO

MIA. Milan Illustrations Agency

LAYOUT

Bayle Graphic Studio

FIRST PRINTING: NOVEMBER 2000

Copyright © 1995 by Master Books
for the CBA U.S. edition.

For information write: Master Books, P.O. Box 727, Green Forest, AR 72638.

ISBN: 0-89051-327-9

ÉDITIONS
DU SIGNE
© ÉDITIONS DU SIGNE 1998